I0410479

Ms. Good-Enough

by
Valerie Gregory, Ed. D.

authorHOUSE™

1663 LIBERTY DRIVE, SUITE 200
BLOOMINGTON, INDIANA 47403
(800) 839-8640
WWW.AUTHORHOUSE.COM

First published by AuthorHouse 04/25/05

ISBN: 1-4208-4290-0(sc)

Printed in the United States of America
Bloomington, Indiana

This book is printed on acid-free paper.

Acknowledgements

This book is dedicated to the love of my life. The one I have been blessed to complete. He says, "All women are special in their own little way."

To my mother Delores Brown Gregory and to my surrogate mothers Veronica Jeannie Byrd, Catherine Lee and Betty White Meadows. To my grandmother Mae Ella Nicholson Gregory and my sisters, Melodie, Angela, Serena, Crystal, and my niece Brittney. I love and respect you all.

Lastly, to my late grandmother, Delores Brown, and both of my greatgrandmothers, Mary Estella Gregory and Ivory Brown.

A special thank you to my aunts Marlena Gregory, Peggy Gregory Newman, Suzanne Gregory and Dolline Knowles.

Table of Contents

Introduction

This book is written to enlighten every female fortunate to be a member of this gender class. Do you realize how many sperm cells are released to determine the sex of every child and they all start out as female. However, only one prevailed to bless you with the crown of femininity. At work one day I was sitting at my desk and one of the students in the hall called out to his teacher, "Ms. Goodenough." A bell went off in my head. He kept calling her until she responded. It was like God was saying to me, "All women are <u>Good-Enough</u>." It's ironic the teacher referenced was engaged to be married and was looking forward to getting her name changed. I talked with her later to say, even when her name changed, always remember she was Good Enough. Before getting married and would always be.

At this same school, I was responsible for psychological evaluations of the student body. One of the males referred for evaluation was a nine year-old third grade student. Before every evaluation, I try to get to know the child and build rapport with them. This particular male was very pleasant and open to conversation. As our talk progressed he told me, "I bet there is something I do you don't think, I do". Of course I asked him what was that. He said, "I date." That jarred my imagination. I asked him to explain. And he went on to say he liked a girl he had known since kindergarten. As he continued the list grew to another three girls all of which were in the third grade. Then he added he liked the sister of one of these girls, and she was in fifth grade. He had been referred because since the beginning of that school year he had been acting out and the teacher was not sure why. He was being sent to in school suspension and was due to see a physician. In a matter of a few minutes just talking to him, I found out that going to in school suspension gave him the opportunity to see these girls. Of course, I had to go and check out who these girls were. I couldn't believe what I saw. The first girl mentioned was of his same ethnicity, the other three were of another ethnicity. And the sister of the first girl was his same ethnicity. I mentioned all of this because none of these girls had breast, or were developed physically. They didn't have on makeup, or have long nails, or not very long hair, or had blonde hair with blue eyes. And they all wore uniforms. The average woman thinks beauty is defined by one of these things. These are just some of the things most females decide that make them more desirable. Yet without any of these so-called assets, he loved them all. This was an immediate wake up call for me. Before I continue, please know I realize beauty is in the eye of the beholder.

But beyond this, he knew females were different and he liked that. None of the girls looked alike, they were all quite different. Yet when he mentioned them his eyes sparkled. When I met the girls they were kind of oblivious to being so admired. By the end of my last session with him he told me that he had gotten the first girl's phone number and she refused his calls and notes. But his determination seemed to win her over; his last report was that she was receiving his calls and that he would be going on a date with her soon. It was so funny to me. He was doing every thing to get these girl's attention. But the girl's didn't see themselves as that special. The young man had a very high IQ, but for our purposes here I want to emphasize, he was like all other males/men, that realize the world without females ain't worth living. So why don't we females realize our value?

Chapter 1-Wonderful and don't know it

When I think of the young man in the introduction and his fascination with the girls mentioned, I wondered did the girls realize how special they were. Of the many girls and women counseled it boggles my mind to hear them express displeasure with themselves. They couldn't see themselves as the rare, unique, heavenly creatures they were. I find most women feel bad about themselves because they tend to compare themselves with other females. And they focus on external things they may not have or don't think they have. How sad is that. Every woman should be her own standard. There is no scale known to man that can measure your greatness. Only you can determine what that is. Thomas Edison said, "If we did all the things we are capable of, we would literally astound ourselves." I want you to think about that for a moment. You have the ability to astound yourself. Why waste your time doing anything else, like comparing yourself to any one. I've heard it said many women don't do better because they don't know better. I think that is partially true. I think the reality is they don't expect better because they don't realize they are better and deserve better. This can be for many different reasons. The root to self-doubt is important but more importantly, one must replace self-doubt with self-love, self-respect and self-acceptance. When a woman does not accept her greatness she is impressed by anything and will usually accept anything.

It is sad that we as women believe we are less than on any level. We are the only ones designed to nurture mankind. There is nothing about us that is less than. If anything, we are extraordinary. Do you know how many sperm cells fought to create the beautiful creation that you are? I am even more awed by the order in which we are born. I for example was born the first in my family to start the next generation. There were no children in the family before I was born. So I was the first child, grandchild, great grandchild, niece, etc. So not only am I female I began the next generation. Can't you see how amazing that is? You too were born female at a particular time because there is something you must do in the earth that only you can do. I am the eldest of five girls. I often thought I wanted a brother. But I realize now, if a brother was needed for me to be successful in life, God would have given me one. I realize all the equipment I need to be successful has been provided for. I tend to be a lot more logical that the average woman because emotionality was not an option afforded me. I like this though. I tend to move on with life a little better than others because of this. That's only because what I was created to do, will not allow me the opportunity to dwell on the unnecessary or what cannot be changed. I take little for granted as a result of this. But this is how I am. What about you, your personality type? What makes you tick and makes you wonderful? This chapter is entitled "Wonderful and don't know it". I would say the average woman has never really keyed into her own uniqueness. Well, my goal in this writing is to make sure you do this right now for the first time. And commit to continually doing so the remainder of your life. We all will continue to evolve all our lives. Or at least we should. What a shame to have lived and to only have existed. My goal every year is to be a better me. Notice each year you get older and you have to deal with changes that might not always be so desirable. Yet you should still be better than you were the year before. There is really no excuse for not being your wonderful self. No one can out beat you being you. The problem is we are trying to be somebody else or somebody we think we ought to be. I have a sister who I say is the sweetest person I know. I admit I am kind but I am not sweet. I don't try to be. That is not my personality. I appreciate my sister's way but I do not try to be like her. I have to be myself. I live within the personality type I have and therein thrive. Notice, I said thrive. You will only thrive when you tap into your own greatness, gifts, and personality. I'm a very organized person, self-motivated and task oriented. I used these gifts to produce and publish my own books. I didn't wait to get inspired, I got up and wrote the books found a publisher and put up the necessary funds. Was it easy? No. Was it workable? Yes. Did it take a long time? Yes. Was it worth it? Yes. You will have to ask yourself some hard questions and answer them honestly. Actually this was the hardest of all the works I had to write. I was ready to publish another book but had committed to publishing this book also. I was given a discount for doing so. So in essence I had to force myself to write and complete the work a lot sooner that I had originally intended too. Did my life stop? No. I had all my regular responsibilities, but I didn't give myself the excuse to not finish the book. You are reading this now because I told myself I have to produce it. What do you have inside of you that you have yet to produce? Don't forget the best gift you can give yourself is self-discovery. Once you are in tuned to you, share your seeds of greatness. God has entrusted you with certain gifts for a reason.

Much of what I write about comes out of my developing as a female daily. No two of us is the same and no two of us will experience life in the same way. In this fact alone, you have something to share that is unknown to another. I currently am employed as a school psychologist/psychological examiner. My entire job is based in this simple principle alone. My job is to discover a person's strengths and weaknesses. The goal becomes to identify their strengths and help my clients work towards developing them and not focus on their weaknesses. I have worked with identical twins whose strengths were not the same. So I know first hand how rare each of us is. I was chosen to write this book because I know each of us is Good Enough and none of us is better than the other nor can we replace another. I am amazed at how one person can be so awesome in one skill and not so awesome in another. This helps me to know the lesser skill was not as important in this person's reason for being here. I know if you really need something it's within you, not outside of you. Each of these people function well enough from day to day to make it. Even intellectually deficient people have something they can do. Even, if it's a smile. I remember one young man who had several mental disabilities who was able to dance really well. The entire student body at this particular middle school supported that. When he would dance at school functions, the whole student body would cheer him on. If you are reading this, what excuse do you have? He danced for the school. What will you do for mankind? I guess the day I realized this, it came somewhat late in life, but none-the-less, it came. The reality is I needed all those experiences before this writing to produce this writing. So it is never too late. I hope you don't let another day go by without you accepting your difference and making the world a better place because of it. If you don't have it, you don't need it. And if you have it, whatever it is. WORK IT GIRL!!!

The great thing about my job is, I can go into every case blind. By this I mean I let every case amaze me. I try not to go into anything with any prejudice of any kind. This is the key to my success. I let every client reveal themselves to me and in turn they learn themselves. I've worked with numerous ages and ethnicity and have come to love diversity and the need for it, all the more. So wonderful one, get with it and amaze your self. Astound your self and then share.

Chapter 2 –Different is good, and its for a reason

I'd like to begin this chapter with an example. Think about this statement: "The moment you are impressed by a man, is the moment you can't help him." A man needs a woman to help him. That is why God created us. A man needs a woman who will accept him as he is but won't allow him to stay that way. She will always push him to do more. If you don't know how valuable you are, you won't push yourself, let alone anyone else. Men need women to help them grow and develop, from birth to old age, from school to career. **I tell my man. "Go out there baby and amaze yourself again. Mama knows you can do it."** The reality is a man needs a wife, a mother and a lover in you. The woman who can maintain this balance will have no problem getting and keeping a man. In every female is the capacity to complete or help her man achieve the things he needs to achieve. These are the qualities of a wife. In every female is a nurturing, and affirming nature that the male gender needs. These are the qualities of a mother. A man will also need to know you can be this for the children he sees you bearing for him, too. And lastly, in every woman is the capacity to be a free, uninhibited female in tuned with her sexuality and the need to share this. Her physical makeup: of breasts are there to feed both her man and her children. Her womb is to house the male genital to allow procreation and a safe place for her child to grow. Remember, woman came out of man. The two main physical parts that were removed from him he still needs to survive. Notice I said to survive, because he literally needs them to survive. He's not an animal or a freak of nature. He is only after what he needs to survive. Which are breasts and her vaginal/womb area. They excite him because they were once apart of him. I heard one man say he could live without food but could never live without sex. Be mindful this does depend on the age of the man, his physical condition, etc. The point is he needs to touch and needs to be touched by a female. With the survival mode explained, you can now understand why they need it so much. Notice again I said need it. I did not say want it. Yes, they want it too. But this is in a category all to itself. A man who is fulfilled sexually is less likely to stray, get in trouble, or be unproductive as a whole. When a man is satisfied sexually, he is rejuvenated to do what he was designed to do. Which is to create, subdue and produce. Think about it ladies, when you are provided for, feel secure, feel loved, and understood, you look for ways to help, nurture and are more likely to be very loving physically. This is how you view love, and sex is how men view love.

So you see it's a cycle: we love on him and he provides for us security. He needs you and you need him. Yes, we came out of him so we need him too. His leadership and visionary mindset give to us something to assist. A woman without the covering of a man is technically naked and unashamedly afraid. We were not designed to cover ourselves. Oh yes, we can do the things men can do, but we still cannot make ourselves feel safe and loved. There is a difference between being loved and loving yourself. You should definitely love yourself but being loved is from without yourself. This is given by another usually a male, we need in our lives. I always say there is nothing like having a tenor speak into your present to make you look toward your future. Feeling loved for each of us can be different. Finding out your love language and your man's love language is a must in order for any relationship to work well. Say for example your love language is to receive gifts but your man communicates his love through verbal affirmation. You will somehow not feel loved. So make an effort to teach your mate your love language and learn there's. My man loves touch, quality time and words. So I shower him with plenty. I make sure he never leaves my presence without his love tank full. My love language he has learned as well. And let me say, Mama is very happy.

Just listen to some of the statements men have made about you beautiful female you. One said if you only knew the power of what you are sitting on. Another said there is no way to explain how good it feels to be inside a woman (no substitute for it). Men love to make love. A man is turned on by a woman's derriere. Sex so good makes you want to come back for more. Notice none of these statements distinguished any particular female from any other. Race, age, size, length of hair or the like made any difference. This literally means every female has the power to gain the attention of a male, solely based on her physical frame alone. She is able to whew any man she chooses to give herself too, because of it. The reality is men can't live without it (sex), unless they are a eunuch. And the female gender is the only creature physically designed to meet this need. They come through the life canal and their male member seeks the comforting surroundings it brings. They were built to go back to where they came from. The problem is women have cheapened the value of this life-giving gem. Most women don't realize its value or its power. When a woman comes to realize its magical or mystical powers if you will, she won't likely cheapen it's value again. Listen ladies if you don't value it, they will use it, because they need it, and disrespect you for it. What you respect, they will respect. And note they will work hard for it. I try to encourage women to think of it, in these terms, if your man wouldn't do it to his daughter, why would you let him do it to you, if he's not your husband, he has no vested interest from which to withdraw. And if he would do it to his daughter like: verbally abuse her, molest her, emotionally torment her, or not provide for her, he's not a man anyway. He needs to grow up away from you.

Woman you are an investment that every man needs to put time and effort into, in order to get a proper rate of return. Ask any man in business, he will tell you he works hard to close a deal and works even harder to keep a deal. You are the greatest deal your man will ever close. He will invest in you and he will make withdrawals frequently. The key ladies, is you will have to make sure his investments yield big dividends. We women are designed to take things and make them better. We are the ones that turn houses into homes. We are the ones who change groceries into meals. So you have your work cut out for you ladies. But you were built to improve what your man brings to you as an investment. Actually, no man wants a woman that is not already producing something. He needs to see some examples in your life of how you took nothing and made something out of it, before he is usually going to make an investment in you. I'm amazed at the women or people who think that if you hope hard enough things will change. No, you will have to do things yourself for things to change. Even the weakest of us can produce something.

That should let everyone know they can produce something, because we all have something to work with. And once you produce anything, you know you can always do it again.

Something that you are will cause an employer to want to hire you. You will bring something to the table that will benefit that company. This is how a relationship should be. The woman will bring her gifts and talents to the table/relationship, if you will, and make the union a better entity because of it. Invest in yourself enough to find out what you can do as a female to make your whole existence better. The wealthy only invest in what they believe will bring them gain. You are an investment that you must be responsible enough for to ensure a gain is received, maintained, and increased. Invest in you and see what will happen.

One thing many women miss is that their difference is what will make all those they come into contact with better. This is a powerful point. It's your difference that makes you valuable. Your sameness discounts you. If someone else can do what you are doing at the same level, the other is unnecessary. That is why when companies begin to merge with other entities, they layoff people that hold similar positions. They make sure that the consolidated organization has every skill necessary for the company to succeed and eliminate anything or one that is redundant. I have been displaced or laid off. It hurt at first, but when I began to understand the thinking behind the change, I fed off of it. I now understand how business evaluates what is profitable overall. It was these experiences that caused me to start my own company. I began my company and other endeavors with this thought in mind: how can my skills be utilized, yet different and still supply the needs of others. Some call this your niche. I challenge you to find out what makes you different and embrace this truth. You will need to look at your strengths, weaknesses, gifts, talents, and devise a plan that will cause you to profit and shine, being your own wonderful self. It is so amazing to me how you draw to your self the other parties that are necessary for you to succeed. But the point/problem is you have to get started. As you put action to your ideas and learn as you go, you will develop skills you didn't know you had. I never saw myself as an author. But I knew I had something to say. I would encounter so many wonderful people and learn so many things that writing them down became a mandatory thing to do. You begin to discover yourself in this way. You begin to appreciate your difference, the differences in others, their gifts and talents as well. It teaches you that we are all different for a reason, that this is good, and we need each other to move forward.

In any organization you have a leader, co-leaders, developers, sustainers, etc. They are all there for a reason. A company can't stand with just a leader, just as one cannot stand with just sustainers. They all exist to make sure the whole company functions properly. The next time you try to be like someone else, think again. I didn't say not to admire the gifts of another. What I am saying is, don't try to be like them or imitate them. Even if you have a mentor and we all should, you should not try to be them. You will always bring a new spin to what you have learned. That's why we all are so beautiful. We can all teach something and we are teaching someone something whether we know it or not. And we all should be learning something. I always say as long as you are still here and your brain works, you can learn something. Surround yourself with knowledgeable people and feed each other. **I warn you be wise enough to know the difference between the time to learn and the time to teach.** You can avoid a lot of pitfalls in life by just following this simple rule. I'm very fortunate that I was born the first of the next generation in my family. All my teachers early in life were adults. For this reason, I believe I have always sought out adults with wisdom to counsel with. So I tend to be a listener more than a talker. It's more important to me to speak when it will benefit the hearers and I can't do that if I haven't listened well. Many of my peers are not my mentors, persons older than myself are. And when they can't speak to a subject that concerns me, I seek out others with wisdom in a particular area. Mind you, you will have to learn how to separate the fish from the bones, in terms of what or whom you will learn from. But the point is, go out there and find out what you want or need to know. Don't make excuses for not achieving your goals. Learn how to put all things into there proper perspective. **Wisdom says work on you, an accept others.** This will help you have fewer stressful days. The reality is you can only change you. So do what you can, be your best self and others will seek you out for it. I can't tell you how many years, I hoped for this or that. Now, I know my, this or that is dependent on me. Say for example you want to start your own business. Go to those who have begun their own business. Research your business options. Go to the library. In general, do your homework, and then move out. I tried various things, before I got where I am. Each situation was a learning experience and I was wiser the next time I stepped out. It is not easy to make a dream a reality. And it is even harder to maintain a dream. Stretching ourselves is what each of us must do. Or we will live and die unfulfilled. Yes, you will run into bumps in the road. But your ultimate goal is to realize your potential in every way and this will cost you. There is no way around that. What will you do? Will you sit around and let life happen? Or will you accept your difference and learn to profit for it. Get up, get going, and Work it girl!!!

Chapter 3-A woman's most valuable asset

Close your eyes. Think about you. Just you. What do you really think about yourself? Do you think you are pretty? Do you think you are ugly? Do you think you are too fat, just right, skinny? Do you think you wish you were someone else? Do you wish you were, whatever? Now think to yourself. Do these thoughts define who you are? What do you define as your greatest asset? Is it your hair, intellect, personality, etc.? Well, the reality is you may be many different things, but ultimately you are a female. And this is your truest asset. Females are the only ones that can do things that no other gender or species can do, like bear children, breast feed, or comfort her fellow man. This is just a small list of the things an amazing female is capable of. So even if you may be in your mind unattractive or slightly overweight, you are still necessary. Your softness is needed in the earth. I would have to say most women are beyond priceless in relationships. They actually are the ones who build the foundation of unity necessary for a relationship to survive. Don't get me wrong it does take two to make a relationship work. But the majority of the maintaining of a wholesome relationship rests with a strong female.

In my job, I run into so many opportunities to learn how mankind functions. And what is so great is that it starts early in our lives not late. When we see children playing they are already developing relational skills. I had a very bright third grade male student that just loved girls. He liked one girl so much, that he found out her phone number without her knowing and pursued her like any adult male would a woman. He would even go out of his way to get in trouble so he could be removed from class in hopes of seeing her. Guess what. She told him she didn't like boys that got in trouble. What do you thing he did? He stopped getting in trouble. Notice a woman voiced what she didn't like and the male who adored her made the adjustment. It's just like that with mothers and their sons. Rebellion does occur because a young man has to find his way. But he will do so trying to get the attention of another female. So women motivate him to be, period. When a man does whatever, some woman somewhere influenced him in someway to do it. The sad part is many women do not realize the power of their influence and leave many men unaware of how to produce. Men tend to be visionaries but they need support and assistance in becoming, so to speak. This is why a woman's influence helps a man to achieve. Say a man wants a son. He can't have one without a woman's assistance.

Sons who do not have good relationships with their mothers deep down resent women as a whole. They will interact with women but their dysfunction will lead them on many roads that often end in self-destruction. I would say neglect or absence counts for a majority of the dysfunction in society. But it doesn't have to be that way. We reach out and are hurt, we reach out again, and the same thing happens. What is the answer? It is not all that simple but it is possible to learn. There is an old Jewish proverb that says, before every child is born, they are aware of why they are. Then an angel at birth kisses them and causes them to forget. The child is required from that day forward to discover why. Each of us was born for a reason or a purpose. In this journey to discover why we are, we will encounter many things that will lead us to that discovery. Embrace your now as you develop yourself to receive your future.

With all that said, let's get to the heart of the matter. Most women want the attention of another, usually a man. The following realizations I have found help women to tap into the power of their femininity and obtain the relationship they want.

I say a woman's most valuable asset is not her lips, breasts, hips, intelligence, etc., but her mouth.

Meaning the words she chooses to use, when she uses them and how she uses them. One of the wisest statements I have ever heard was from my surrogate father, Nathaniel King. He said, "A woman can make or break a relationship with her <u>ivory box</u>." Her mouth. I have made that statement, apart of my male language knowledge base. Men speak and women speak but not often enough to each other in a way the other understands. So women must begin early in a relationship to understand her man's language and adjust her powerful gift of words to accomplish an expected end. A happy home. I often say a man listens a whole lot more to a woman who touches him softly with her words. If you don't believe me try the opposite and see what happens. Most men communicate nonverbally. Study your man's nonverbal cues or signals, and respond accordingly. A little boy will likely ask for a hug. Your man may just come up to you and take one (a hug). He asked you the same thing, just nonverbally.

When I call men by their last name, how they receive my words. That simple act of respect will get any woman noticed. I have found men really respond to the words of others so readily. The tone, the words, the reference and the relationship between them and the receiver are inseparable. One man said if you want to make a man, bring a woman into his life. And if you want to destroy a man, bring a woman into his life. Much of what he was trying to say is that what a woman says and does will either make or break a man. Men are very attentive to the words of a woman. And with this a woman must use her words wisely are bear the brunt of not enjoying him. Men who do not feel appreciated or supported eventually leave their female companion. So ladies in this chapter the focus is on this reality, you speak your man's destiny in your life as either positive or nonexistent. Men believe the words of the woman they have chosen to listen too. When I worked at a distribution center, I learned quickly men are not hard to talk too and will open up and talk to anyone they feel comfortable around.

So when I hear women say, men do not talk, I say to them they haven't been listening. They have been talking, but not listening. I also learned men fall in love a lot quicker than we women. Most men have made up their minds about the type of relationship they want to have with a female long before the female ever picks up on what he is looking for. Women realize when a man is making such decisions your words and deeds have already made an impact. **I always say a woman can win or lose a man by her words, way, and wisdom.** The good thing about this is that every woman is so unique we can't copy cat another. So it behooves you to find out what words, and way, applied in wisdom coincide with your unique personality. We will talk about this more in later chapters, but for now realize the heart of a woman is largely displayed in these two main areas: her words, and her way.

So in review think about what you are creating when you speak. The world you are presently living in reflects all the words you have ever spoken. Ladies please don't think that I am implying that you should not voice your opinions. All I'm saying is, think before you speak, check your attitude, stick with the subject at hand and watch your tone. Many victories or defeats lie in this awesome truth. When men are spoken too, if they feel they are being attacked, they will shut down. But if they are made to feel you are expressing an opinion that is valid in a non-judgmental manner your words are more likely to be heard and responded too positively. And in reality this is what we really want. Men have listened to women all their lives and they value our words. You will have to determine if he will listen to you. This small reality resulted in my being proposed to when I had not really even known a guy. This young man was introduced to me by phone through a distant relative. We only spoke on the phone, due to living in different states. He was in the military and I was working and attending graduate school. It was my birthday present from him to me. I declined because I wasn't ready. Just by watching the words I said and the way I expressed myself I received a proposal sight unseen. So ladies you can't convince me words don't matter. As Daddy King once said, a woman can make or break a relationship with her ivory box (her mouth). You can tear down something that took twenty years to build in a matter of seconds because of this principle. He also said a woman should seduce a man's mind before she seduces his body because once she has seduced his mind, she will always have his body. And one of the best ways to do this is, with your words, spoken in the right way, at the right time.

A man falls in love with the essence of the woman. I have asked many men questions about what drew them to the women in their lives and the resounding answer is always, how she makes me feel when I'm with her. And the quickest and most powerful way to touch a man is with your words.

One of my biggest revelations was the gift of silence. When I learned to listen and when to speak, it made life so much simpler. I found men became attracted to my quiet nature. A woman who is content with her self sees no need to prove points are to convince others of her belief: she just lives what she believes. I find this consistent response wins the respect of males and females alike. It does not mean when you are silent that you agree or that your opinion is not important, it merely means you choose not to comment. You have that right. Wisdom comes in here. Wisdom should direct whether or not a statement should be made. Each statement should clarify and benefit the hearers but more importantly convey what must bo revealed in an encouraging way. One's attitude or tone is crucial when attempting to convey an opinion. All can be lost in this realm alone. Years of trust can be lost with a few words, spoken in the wrong tone. Please, please, think before you speak. We look at those in prison found guilty of murder in disbelief and judgment, yet we commit murder to the spirit of our hearers whenever we speak words of death into their lives. Think about it. Who has spoken words of death to your inner spirit. And more than that who have you spoken words of death too. After you reflect on this thought, determine in your heart not to be a murderer another day. This is a huge task, yet a manageable one. I live my life by this principle, and I am getting better every day. I hope this work will encourage you that your humanness is not fatal, but rather a life-giving event, where daily one can produce more pleasant memories instead of damnable ones.

I heard a man say men are very comfortable with a woman who touches him with her words, and touches him with her ways, and gives him space to just be and rest. But if you think about it, we are all like that. A Big Mama who says the right thing, in her own way, allowing for privacy, for the receiver, is priceless. I'm trying to let you see what you can respect and desire is already in you. Give what you want to receive. Remember no one who is smothered can grow.

The great thing about being a single person is that you get time to really look at your life, your idiosyncrasies and come to terms with them. You learn how to live within the parameters of just being human. It's amazing how understanding one can be of others when you realize you have faults as well. How would you feel if you where not appreciated, understood, or valued? More than likely resentful. That is the effect you have on others when you don't monitor your words, or ways in wisdom. So let's review, What do the four w's stand for? Words, Way, with Wisdom.

Before I conclude this chapter, I want to encourage every woman to learn her man's love language. Some men say few words; others say many. But the key is that he feels comfortable enough to open up to you when he does decide to talk. Be very attentive to what he may or may not be saying. This is a extremely critical point to be understood, especially when you both are experiencing tough times. In tough times, men tend to go within themselves. They tend to need time alone to think things through. It doesn't mean he's shutting you out. It just means he's trying to gain some since of control. Hopefully, your man has men friends or mentors they feel comfortable enough with to talk too. Either way, it is at this time it is more important you be a helper to him by allowing him his space. Please, please, only speak when necessary. And above all else do not demand things of him or nag. When a man is trying to feel his way, your nagging only causing him to want to leave you out of his world all together. And this is not what you want. Some things you will not be able to help him with. But just him knowing you are there, when he decides to share, will be more than enough. And realize he may decide not to share. And that is okay. I talked with a man who had a bad day at work. Before I knew it, he was unloading all of his frustrations. I didn't counsel him; I just listened. I prayed while he spoke and hoped to speak only what would help him. My aim was only to make him feel heard. A few weeks later he called me for assistance with a project. I went out of my way to help him. I told him like I had always before; I would do what I could. Fortunately, things worked out. Later in one of our conversations, he said he knew whom to call. I said it is good to know that you can be counted on. This response only came out of my being consistent and understanding. Any man will run to a woman who is consistently there for him and understanding of him. He was not even my male companion. This love language is universal. When he's ready to talk, let him be heard and let your God given intuitive nature encourage him in the way he needs it most. Let me caution you, this cannot be done without God's aid. Men and women speak too different languages but God knows the language of both. He knows what you don't and He knows what your man needs, so lean on the creator for assistance in these matters. **Seek not to understand him all the time but seek to accept him all of the time.** There will be times when you will need to listen, other times you will need to scold, and yet other times when you will need to express an opinion, etc. For each time, God will know the delivery that is best.

Lastly, every man loves you to call him pet names. I have always given people pet names. It is just who I am. My father hates nick names, however he loves the one I have given him. Any term of endearment says to your man you are so, so, so, special to me. They want to always know you feel more for them than any other man on the planet and nothing says this better than your love names. I worked with a teacher that called all of her children Lovely. She would say do this Lovely, come here Lovely, etc., she taught middle school aged learning-disabled children. No matter which child she was speaking to, they all responded to her request, boy or girl. Somehow they knew which Lovely she was talking too. It was wonderful to watch. I have called children from kindergarten through high school aged: sweetheart, sweetness, baby, beautiful one, etc. and they too all respond positively. We all respond to positive loving names. For those closest to me, I make up names. I have given my sister's dog some twelve different names in the last two years and he responds to every one. You should know if an animal responds to a positive love name, your man will. The day you have no love name for your significant other be warned bitterness has set in.

Lastly, I want to tell you what I tell my man every chance I get: "Go out there baby and amaze yourself again!" Find a phrase that will inspire your man. He should know beyond a shadow of doubt, <u>you believe in him</u>.

Chapter 4-Who told you, you weren't good enough

All of us have had unpleasant experiences we can point to that may have harmed our view of ourselves in some way. If it didn't happen in your home or initial environment, life will provide such experiences at school, work, play, etc. Each of us will run into a bully along the way. Someone so wounded, they live to find fault in the world and in all those they encounter along the way. <u>The reality is, wounded people, wound people.</u> The hope is when a negative or untrue reality is presented to you; you do not make it your reality. By this I mean, say those you love the most a mother, father, brother, sister, teacher say something to you that makes you feel less than on any level for any reason. You may feel hurt and that is common but do you go beyond this and assume it to be true. Whatever you assume to be true of you; becomes your reality. For example, somebody said to you, your sister is way prettier than you. You won't ever get a boyfriend. What do you do with such a statement, in your mind, what do you say to yourself about yourself. Do you say, "That's right she is way prettier than I am, I don't think I'll ever have a boyfriend"? What you decide to accept turns out to be what you expect. If someone finds you attractive, you might disagree mentally because you agreed with the statement made earlier. "I'm not attractive as so and so and I won't ever have anyone to want me as a girlfriend." You will subconsciously push people away because you now believe you are undesirable and not worthy of another's attention. This is a sad state to live it. It's a state that is based on a lie that ultimately becomes your reality. Many fall prey to such statements presented to them in life and live stunted lives because of it. It doesn't have to be this way. You have to do decide what reality you will have for yourself. Others don't make that decision, you do. That is kind of hard to take. But it's the truth. Yes, they were wrong for the things they did and said. And yes that person should have protected you and made you feel safe. They didn't do what they should have. Now what do you do. Do you live your life as a victim to their faulty view of you, or do you decide to view yourself from the perspective of I'm the only person on this planet that can change the world the way I was born to do. Yes, you were born to do something extraordinary. And the universe will not be what it can be without your influence and input. So what are you going to do? Live beyond potential and make it a hard reality or live life aimlessly without purpose because you chose less for yourself.

I would have to say the majority of my cases stem from this chapter's topic. "Who told you, you weren't good enough?" But more importantly, why did you choose to believe it. I had to dedicate a chapter of this book specifically to women regarding this thought, because women were the first people, fed this lie. In the Bible, it says Eve, the first woman, was tempted by the serpent. Who caused her to doubt her significance and place in the world. He caused her to question herself so much, that she chose the option he presented. Which was that she was not significant. But the reality was, she was significant all a long. She didn't need anything outside of herself to be great. She was already great. Life and circumstances for many women have caused them since this event to doubt themselves in some way. This is where the whole thinking of, I'm not good enough began. This lie is so powerful, that thousands of years later; women still doubt themselves. This aught to tell you how valuable a woman must really be. When a woman does not know her value, she taints every thing in her path. When Eve was confused regarding her value, she swayed Adam to make a bad choice. Because of his love and respect for her, he complied, and they lost everything. Now just think of it, if Eve had never doubted herself, she would have not used her God given influence to destroy the man she was designed to complete or make better. The serpent can take on many different forms for every woman, but none-the-less the objective is always the same, doubt your value and hope for something better. Some women who take this persecution come back with a vengeance to prove others wrong. While others become resentful and bitter, yet others become victims blaming perpetrators for their plight in life. And lastly, still others live with such low self-esteem that they accept no good reality. I would hope that each of you has decided to realize you may have been lied too. And that you can start today, to create the reality you want. Change any negative reality you may be experiencing, by choosing only to believe my outcome is based on my realizing my value can't be defined by anyone, but me. That is to say, I'm greatness, period. I was speaking with a male and it was something to hear him describe me, to me. He said, " I know you can be trusted and if you say something it's from the heart". Now this is true, that what he mentioned was right. But whether he had said it or not, I know that's what kind of person I am. It was nice to hear it, but know it did not validate me. There are many things you should know about yourself whether someone else confirms it or not. Erase all your negative thoughts and replace them with factual thoughts that confirm your value and necessariness. Yes, you are necessary. We need you female, be sure you know that.

I work with young girls all the time who basically dislike themselves. I immediately begin to do what I call "mental surgery". I work on the wrong mindsets the young lady may have about herself an implant good ones (mindsets). One thirteen year-old girl, I served had been adopted at birth. She came from a loving environment yet she still felt not worthy of her family's love. Her feelings of abandonment and rejection had resulted in such low self-esteem that she always held her head down and she walked cowardly and ashamed. The first statement out of her mouth was, "I'm adopted." She might as well said my biological parents didn't think I was worth raising. I knew from her school records that her biological mother had been a drug addict, but that didn't matter. All that she saw was, she was a reject that some family took pity on and had adopted. All I saw was greatness. The first thing I did, was assure her, her family loved and really wanted her. Next, I started a game with her. I said I can't see that beautiful face with your head down. So I'd say the rule is: hold your head up. Whenever I see you and say what's the rule: what should you do? She would hold her head up. Within two days, she was beginning on her own to hold her head up when I saw her. Next, I found out what she was good at. She liked to sew, so I found out information on television, etc. to help develop her interest. The next thing I knew, she was in the school play. I told her I would be sure to come and see her. I still have to remind her from time to time to hold her head up, but she is beginning to do it on her own. See there, that didn't take two hours in all to help that young lady see herself differently. Our breakthrough moment came when she told me she wanted to go to another school because students there spread rumors. I told her, they spread rumors wherever you go. I told her she was going to have to learn the difference between truth and rumor. I said to her, for example, if someone spread the rumor she was fat. Would that be true? She said no, because she was thin. Then I said if someone spread the rumor that she was pretty. Would that be true? Before she could say anything negative, I said that would be true. I had to replace her thoughts of unattractiveness with a reality she couldn't even comprehend. You will have to do this same process for yourself. I've had to do this for myself and am continuing to do it. My grandmother did a similar mindset change with me. One of my relatives is very attractive. I was going on about her, and my grandmother stopped me, mid-sentence and said, yes, she is attractive, but you are classy. I have never forgotten that. My relative is glamorous and I'm classy. I like being classy. It's who I am. I can't be anything else. Neither, do I want too. So get to work. Erase the faulty thoughts in your psyche and replace it with brand new thinking. Negative mindsets lock you up and stifle your potential, just like a virus locks up your computer. Unlock you mind today and open yourself up to all that is positively possible.

Chapter 5-Rediscover the gift within

Now that you have a new mindset, and a new attitude, you are ready to rediscover the gift within.

Growing up what made you happy when you were engaged in it. What came easy to you? Did you have a natural affinity to running? Did you just love being outside and running through your neighborhood? Guess what, this is probably something you were gifted to do and your life's future and passion may be tied to it. Each of us has gifts and talents that were naturally engrained in us before we were born. These instincts we do not have to work up, they just are. If running is your gift, you will likely have to train and prepare, if you should decide to make this a career path. But all of us will have to assess our gifts and talents and put our energies into developing them. Your passion is usually tied to your gifts and financial opportunities in the future. As a female, I realize we tend to discount many of our gifts and talents as we grow. We begin to fall into modes of behavior society may have placed upon us. We live what I call the "I should life." And never end up living the "I would life."

When I was in tenth grade I was in a college preparatory high school. I had no clue of what career path I was going to pursue. I remember asking my chemistry teacher what should I pursue in college. She said to me, "What are you good at?" I said, "Math." She said business would be a good major. Well, with me being the task oriented person I am, I went straight to the business school picked up the degree outline and followed it until I graduated. I completed my degree in three years, which was commendable, but it was not the right career path choice for me. I went to college with the thinking of getting a good job, not the idea of gaining a skill and developing myself thereby. I guess that's why six years after working as an accountant, I walked away from the corporate world. I then began years of self-discovery in vocations and am now writing this book. I would hope you don't have to go around the mulberry bush so to speak, to find your proper vocation. Don't get me wrong; I wouldn't change a thing. I just know things could have gone differently if I had evaluated all of my skills, gifts and talents at that time. I think the thing I love the most about my life is, that it has taught me so much and I adore the wisdom that it has given. I wouldn't trade anything for wisdom. I remember saying to my aunt when I turned a certain milestone in age, that if I knew then at age twenty, the things I know now, I would have been a bad mamma jamma. It's all those experiences that now afford me the opportunity to share, what you are now reading. I present what I write because I know life doesn't have to beat you, to teach you. You can live life and love the journey as you go.

When the young lady in the last chapter mentioned how she loved to sew, I knew that was likely the career path she should pursue. I told her to be sure to bring me her latest creation so I could see it. I kept telling her that there were millions, even billions out there being made every day in the clothing/design industry. Now what about you?

I begin all of my sessions with, tell me something about yourself. What do you like to do? In the first ten minutes are so, I connect with that person and all their interests and greatness begins to unfold. Many people have never even taken the time to ask themselves such questions. They just do what they do and think its normal. Yes, it's normal. It's normal for that person but extraordinary all the same to someone else. I wear clothes everyday but have no desire to sew, let alone design an outfit. Someone else is supposed to do that, while I buy what they have produced. They may one day take the time to buy my book. The point is we can't all be doing the same things. Even in the clothing industry, different outfits will attract different buyers, so you can easily see there is always room for variety. I love all fields of study because each has it's own specialty. You don't go to a dermatologist if you have a cavity. Both a dermatologist and a dentist are doctors, but each services different needs. Look at your self as a specialist that is discovering what your service is to be. Once you make this discovery, hone your skill, develop it and put it on the market. You may have the gift of charisma where people are just naturally drawn to you. You find that company executives seek you out as their public relations representative. This is no coincidence that executives notice this gift in you. They know you can bring business to their organization because of it. So why don't you see each of your gifts in this same way. People of influence are always looking to attach themselves with those who can make their missions successful ones. What a shame for an executive in essence, to see what you do not realize as a gift, use it and prosper because of it, and you end up living an unfulfilled life. Now who is wrong, the executive or you? You know the answer is, you. No more excuses, take out a piece of paper right now and write down all of your strengths, gifts and talents you know you possess. Be honest, make sure they are things you like to do and are things that tend to be easy and natural for you. Ask yourself which of these things would you do even if you weren't paid for doing it? The choice you make can become a vehicle that brings finances to you. Be wise, devise a plan and work your plan. But get going. I had the copyright to my first works three years before I ever found a publisher. When the opportunity presented itself, I was ready. I live my life this way. I work on myself in some way everyday and invariably an opportunity eventually arises, and I jump right in. When I was not working on projects and was living a mundane life, I hated my job. I accepted the status quo and just wondered through most of my days. My income tripled but I was miserable. This is just a reminder money cannot satisfy your hunger to fulfill your purpose. I still do mundane things but I'm not just existing anymore. I'm making my mark every chance I get. I'm not motivated by anything other than this is what I should be doing. I force myself to stretch all the time. Some days I say I just want to live a normal life. But the reality is there is no normal life. Each of us is so unique no two of our lives is to be like the other, so there can be no normal. That's why marriage stretches us all. Marriage requires two unique individuals to live together in their uniqueness and compliment the other. It's this process that changes two people and makes them both better for the common good of the whole. If you are good handling money, develop that skill and help others with it, like your husband in money management. Be sure your gift is appreciated though and don't force it on others or you will cause resentment. All in all, do what you do best and share it. This is how you rediscover the gift within.

Chapter 6-Ms. Good-Enough come forth

I want to begin this chapter with one thought, that I don't want you to ever forget. "You are Good Enough". Say that out loud. Whenever you feel less than or inadequate in any way, please say this to yourself, "I'm Good Enough!"

When we started out on this journey, we established this thought early. Here in this final chapter, we put the hammer on the nail and drive this thought home. Now that this book has been written, I'm challenged with the thought how many women will read this. And more important than that, will they finally get it. I look at how my life has gone and realize this truth is necessary for life no matter what your vocation. We are not to be defined by how we look, feel or others. We are defined by what we think and know about ourselves. Your reality will reflect what you think you know about who you are. For example, I know I should not be disrespected, so I don't accept any disrespect. I know I should be respected, so I only accept those who are up to respecting me. The moment I feel another has lost a perspective that is important to me, I let the other party know and make the necessary adjustments. I don't assume people will know what matters to me. I let them know at the appropriate time what is acceptable or needful. This is good, because in this way we learn how to get along. Many women don't know what they deserve so they accept whatever comes along. But a woman who knows she's Good Enough, sets a standard that others will either accept and understand or will reject. And rejection in this case is good. Because if you choose to lie to yourself about what matters to you, you end up miserable in the long run for settling for less any way. I have learned not to compromise the things that really matter to me. I will be quite honest with you. I have endured some very difficult times, but I have never thought it was necessary for me to prostitute myself in any way. Prostituting oneself can come in many forms and this will vary from person to person. But all I know is, while I was going through those tough times, it was never so bad that I would allow myself to go that route. Somehow, I would always get through those times. I remember at my lowest, I moved from one state back home to my mother's to pursue my graduate education. When I left that state, I promised myself I would never live as a second-class citizen again. I paid my mom $200 a month for rent until I was able to get my own place, two years later. Now as a doctor, I can honestly say I have never lived as a second-class citizen since. This is the one thing I love about people from third world countries. They see life as an opportunity. They recognize they are valuable simply because they are. Most don't value themselves by what they possess, but instead by what they can offer. What an amazing mindset. What do you have to offer Ms. Good-Enough?

I worked during the 1996 Olympics as a volunteer. This was my first experience with many of the ethnicities of the world. I since have traveled to Europe and this has driven this thought home more. We are a global community. We all are important. And our differences are what make our world great. In one of my experiences, I worked at an elementary school where one third of the student body, were first generation immigrants to the United States. It was wonderful. These students were sponges for learning and open to change. When I went overseas, I understood all the more, what sacrifices they were choosing to make for the greater good of their families. The good thing about going to another state to live without any point of reference taught me I needed others to help me get along. I was a stranger in a foreign land, even though it was my own. I tell people now I moved to that place a little girl, but I came back a woman. Now I share this woman with you. I'm Good-Enough and you are too. You bring something else to this world no one else can.

You!!! You are it. And whatever your "**it**" is, Work It!!! I plead with you, Ms. Good-Enough, come forth, we need you.

Ms. Good-Enough

(Chorus)

Who is that girl, lady, woman over there?
Who is that picture of beauty, kindness and
meekness so rare?
Who is that girl, lady, woman that's respected
everywhere?
Who is that girl, lady, woman that makes every
man stop and stare?
They say her name is Ms. Good-Enough
And that's no surprise
Because in every woman, she does abide

She is every where you look
In the grocery store, the office, and a cook
She lives with you and down the street
She is femininity that just can't be beat
She answers those who call, with her gracious
ways
And she touches your soul like no other all of her
days
They say her name is Ms. Good-Enough
And that's no surprise
Because in every woman, she does abide

She is strong and humble when necessary
On her you can depend and not to worry
She knows how to make you feel special
Because she knows you are an original
She doesn't waste time, oh no, never
For if she did, she might regret it forever
They say her name is Ms. Good-Enough
And that's no surprise
Because in every woman, she does abide

Another baby girl was born today
A daughter, future friend and mother
A gem, jewel, priceless creation surpassed by no
other
She looks up into nurturing eyes
Who some day she will comprise
They say her name is Ms. Good-Enough
And that's no surprise
Because in every woman, she does abide

I ask you once again, who's that female?
Who defines all that is woman and can attract
any male
I know who she is
They say her name is Ms. Good-Enough
And that's no surprise
Because in every woman, she does abide

About the Author

The author, Valerie Marie Gregory, is a doctor of education, practicing as a psychological examiner. She is also the author of *The Me in We* and *Understand Him and Keep Him. Ms. Good-Enough* her latest book is dedicated to every female in all her glory. Her aim is to help every female rediscover her beautiful wonderfulness. After years of working in the field of psychology, with both youths and adults, the author concluded that most females have loss their sense of self, identity and true self worth. She felt compelled to write a book to these women who need to rethink, what every woman must realize about herself. Which is, her value is without measure and she needs to start treating herself as such.

The focus of this work is to enlighten every female that her not realizing her true value cheats herself and the world of a divinely unique creature. The title was meant to jar every female that where ever she is in life, she is GOOD-ENOUGH. Most women all of their lives struggle with this thought. Most women think there is something about themselves that doesn't measure up and she deserves less. So this book is to proclaim to all females, you are indeed GOOD-ENOUGH and only accept what you truly deserve. Which is the best. I learned this lesson from a kindergarten student and have never looked back. My hope is after you read this book you will never look back either.